D1717228

PETER PANINI'S CHILDREN'S GUIDE

THE
LIVING TREASURES
OF THE
HAWAIIAN ISLANDS

THE STORY OF HAWAI'I'S NATIVE PLANTS AND ANIMALS

WRITTEN BY STACEY KAOPUIKI
ILLUSTRATED BY STACEY KAOPUIKI AND BOB WAGSTAFF

HAWAIIAN ISLAND CONCEPTS

DEDICATION

Dedicated to my Dad, Solomon, and to others like him,

who have a special place in their hearts

for the native plants and animals of Hawai'i.

Published by Hawaiian Island Concepts
P.O. Box 1069, Wailuku, Maui, Hawaii 96793-1069

Text copyright © 1994 Hawaiian Island Concepts
Illustrations copyright © 1994 Hawaiian Island Concepts

Book design by Wagstaff Design, Maui, Hawaii.

Library of Congress Catalogue Card Number: #94-075646
ISBN #1-878498-04-5

First Printing, December 1994

Second Printing, June 1997

Printed in Hong Kong

Did you know that most of the plants and animals that we see
in Hawai'i today came from other parts of the earth?

It's true. Many are really the plants and animals of other countries that were brought here by man. The plumeria, for example, is a plant from Mexico.

The pineapple is from South America.

The myna bird is from India.

And some researchers believe that even the coconut was brought here by the Polynesians when they arrived.

But there are some plants, insects, birds and other living creatures that are Hawai'i's own. They were living here long before the arrival of man and most cannot be found anywhere else in the world.

Aloha . . . my name is Peter Panini and this is my dog, Punahele. This is the story about the native plants and animals of Hawai'i. Before we begin, there are a few words we need to know:

NATIVE

A plant or animal is called **NATIVE** only if it arrives by natural means, without the help of man. There are two kinds of **NATIVE** plants and animals:

ENDEMIC

When a **NATIVE** plant or animal lives only in a certain place and nowhere else in the world it is called **ENDEMIC**. An example is the **'ĀKOHEKOHE,** a bird that lives only in Hawai'i.

INDIGENOUS

When a **NATIVE** plant or animal lives in a certain place, as well as in other places of the world, it is called **INDIGENOUS**. An example is this **HALA** tree, which grows in Hawai'i, as well as in other places of the Pacific.

4

ENDANGERED

An **ENDANGERED** plant or animal is in real trouble. It means that there are so few of them living that they are very close to extinction.

THREATENED

A **THREATENED** plant or animal are those species that need help to keep them from becoming **ENDANGERED** in the near future.

Both **ENDANGERED** and **THREATENED** species are protected by law to help them survive.

EXTINCT plants or animals are those species we will never see again because they are no longer living. They have vanished from our earth, forever.

Come on, let's begin our story . . .

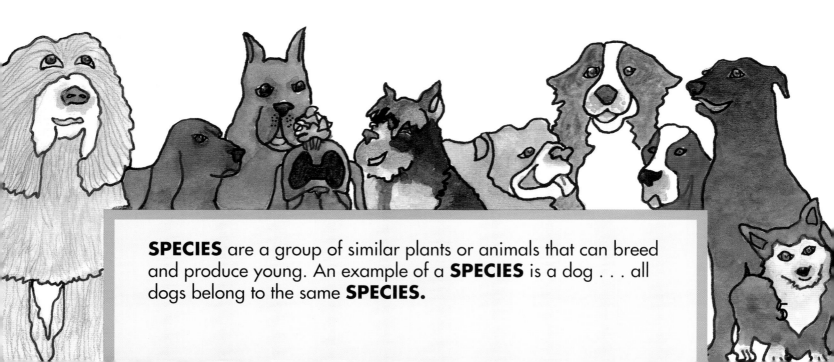

SPECIES are a group of similar plants or animals that can breed and produce young. An example of a **SPECIES** is a dog . . . all dogs belong to the same **SPECIES.**

The Hawaiian Islands were born long, long ago, when powerful, undersea volcanoes rose in the middle of the largest, deepest ocean on earth.

There was no life. The Islands lay barren, silent and still.

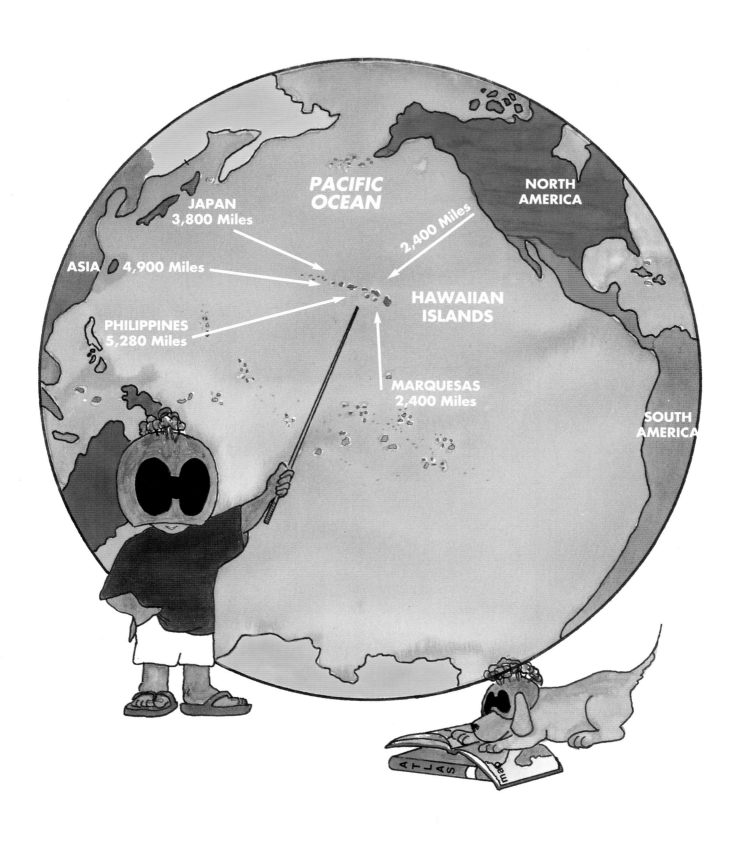

B ut over millions of years a few plants and animals made incredible journeys across the vast Pacific Ocean and landed upon these tiny Islands . . . without any help from man.

Scattered and carried by the forces of nature, tiny seeds, insects, plants, birds and other forms of life came tumbling in the wind, drifting upon the ocean, soaring within huge storms and hitch-hiking on other creatures. It was only by remakable chance that they stumbled upon our Islands. Most were swallowed by the sea.

Only a small handful were able to survive under the hot Hawaiian sun. These species became the first ancestors of all Hawai'i's native plants and animals.

WAGSTAFF

9

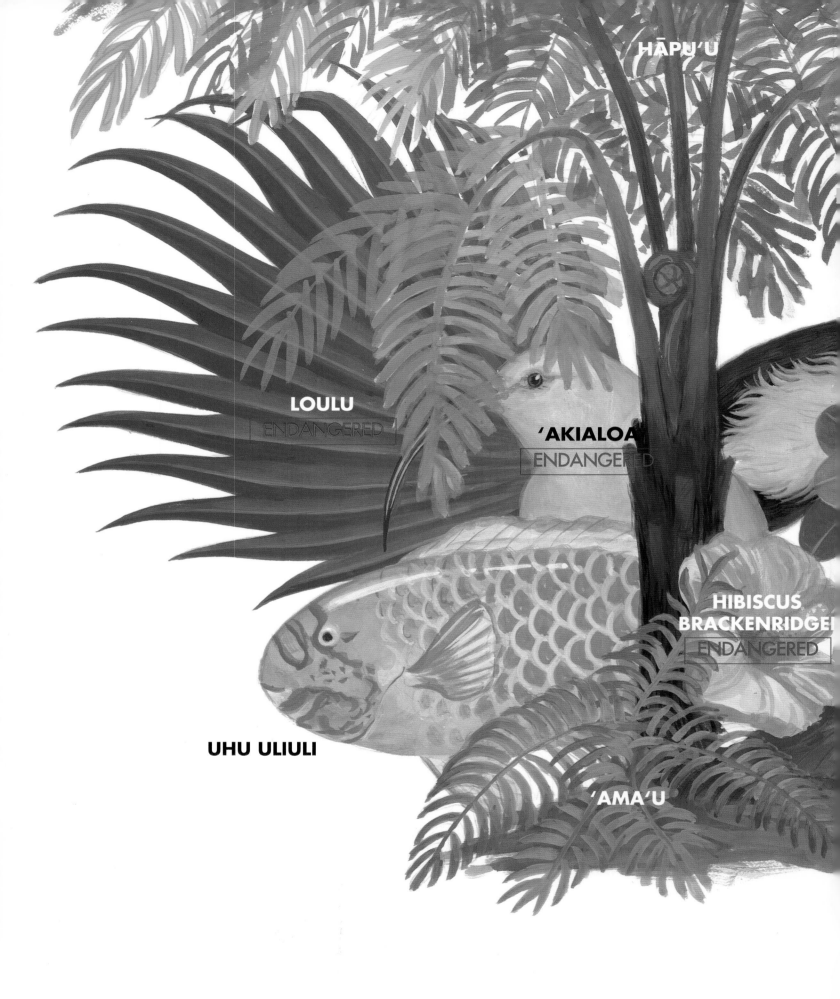

HĀPU'U

LOULU
ENDANGERED

'AKIALOA
ENDANGERED

HIBISCUS
BRACKENRIDGEI
ENDANGERED

UHU ULIULI

'AMA'U

Something amazing slowly happened to many of these plants and animals during thousands of years of living on our far away Islands — they gradually changed themselves!

Tiny insects became giants. Thorny plants lost their thorns. Towering trees became dwarfs. Birds changed colors, the shape of their beaks changed, and they sang different songs. And a few flying insects and birds even stopped flying because they had no enemies.

Some species changed a little, while others changed a lot. The changes helped each species to make better use of the different kinds of food and habitats they found around them. They also created thousands of new plants and animals from the few that first arrived. These new plants and animals did not look or behave like their ancestors, or like any other plant or animal in the world.

They were Hawai'i's own.

Come on, let's meet some of the native plants and animals of Hawai'i.

O'O
EXTINCT

ĀLULA
ENDANGERED

HAWAIIAN DAMSELFLY

ILIAHI
Sandalwood

'ĀKALA
Hawaiian Raspberry

Plants and animals depend upon their shape or design to get food and to survive. Evolution is the slow, gradual process in which a species changes itself to help it survive.

11

This is the **'A'O** and the **'IWA,** two of the many different kinds of seabirds that make their home in Hawai'i.

Seabirds such as the **'A'O** feed on small fish near the ocean's surface. By watching the actions of these seabirds, fishermen can find schools of larger fish that come to feed on the small fish too.

'A'O
Newell's Shearwater
Endemic

Threatened

More than five million seabirds nest in the tiny Islands of the Hawaiian Islands National Wildlife Refuge. It is an important home for many species.

The **'IWA** is a large bird that is often seen soaring near coasts. The Hawaiians call this bird **'IWA,** or thief, because it often steals fish from other seabirds. The **'IWA,** is also a sign to sailors that they are near land.

Because seabirds can live at sea for long periods of time, they had little trouble in reaching Hawai'i.

'IWA
Great Frigatebird
Indigenous

WAGSTAFF

13

See that? That's our Hawaiian monk seal. They love to bask in the sun and are underwater acrobats who can dive down 500 feet or more. These large seals feed on eels, lobsters, octopus and fish.

If you're real lucky you might see a monk seal on the main Hawaiian Islands, but most are found in the remote Islands to the northwest.

ʻĪLIO-HOLO-I-KAUAUA
Hawaiian Monk Seal
Endemic

Endangered

The monk seal has lived on the earth for over 15 million years. Today it and the HONU are fighting for their survival. One way we can help is to stop throwing plastic things into the sea or on the beach, where these animals swallow or become entangled in them.

In the shallow waters of Hawai'i you can also find the **HONU** as it feeds on **LIMU,** or seaweed. This marine reptile always returns to its place of birth to mate and lay its eggs.

HALA
Pandanus
Indigenous

HONU
Green Sea Turtle
Indigenous
Threatened

NAUPAKA
Indigenous

15

WAGSTAFF

Seven different species of waterbirds live in the wetlands of Hawai'i. If we sit real quietly we can watch these three.

The **KOLOA** is the Hawaiian duck. It can be found on all islands except Lāna'i. It feeds on freshwater plants, snails and insects.

The tall, slender bird wading around is the **AE'O.** It is looking for small fish and water insects, which it likes to eat.

KOLOA
Hawaiian Duck
Endemic
Endangered

The darker bird is the **'ALAE 'ULA.** Old Hawaiian legends say that these birds were the fire-keepers who brought fire to the Hawaiians. Many native birds, such as these, have important parts in ancient Hawaiian legends.

Waterbirds, along with certain insects, plants and animals, need water to live and grow in. The Hawaiian wetlands — our marshes, ponds, streams, **LO'I** and mudflats — are very important places for them.

AE'O
Hawaiian Stilt
Endemic
Endangered

'ALAE 'ULA
Hawaiian Common Moorhen
Endemic
Endangered

To help preserve a species we must protect and preserve its' habitat — the place it lives.

WAGSTAFF

MĀMAKI
Endemic

PŪPŪ-KANI-OE
Hawaiian Land Snail
Endemic

Endangered

18

ook over there! It's a Hawaiian land snail on a **MĀMAKI** leaf. These rare jewels of the native forests are famous for the beautiful colors and patterns on their shells.

Although they are called land snails, some actually live on the leaves of native plants and trees.

The Hawaiians used plants in many different ways. The small fruit that you see on the **MĀMAKI** was used for medicine, while the plant's bark was peeled, soaked, beaten and dried into **KAPA**, a bark cloth that had many uses.

From just a few snails who landed here, more than 1000 different species of land snails evolved in Hawai'i.

WAGSTAFF

This unusual creature is the **HĪHĪWAI.** It lives in the cool, freshwater streams of Hawai'i, but it begins life as tiny larva that are swept from these streams into the salty sea.

Exactly what happens at sea is still a mystery, but while at sea the larva changes into tiny **HĪHĪWAI.**

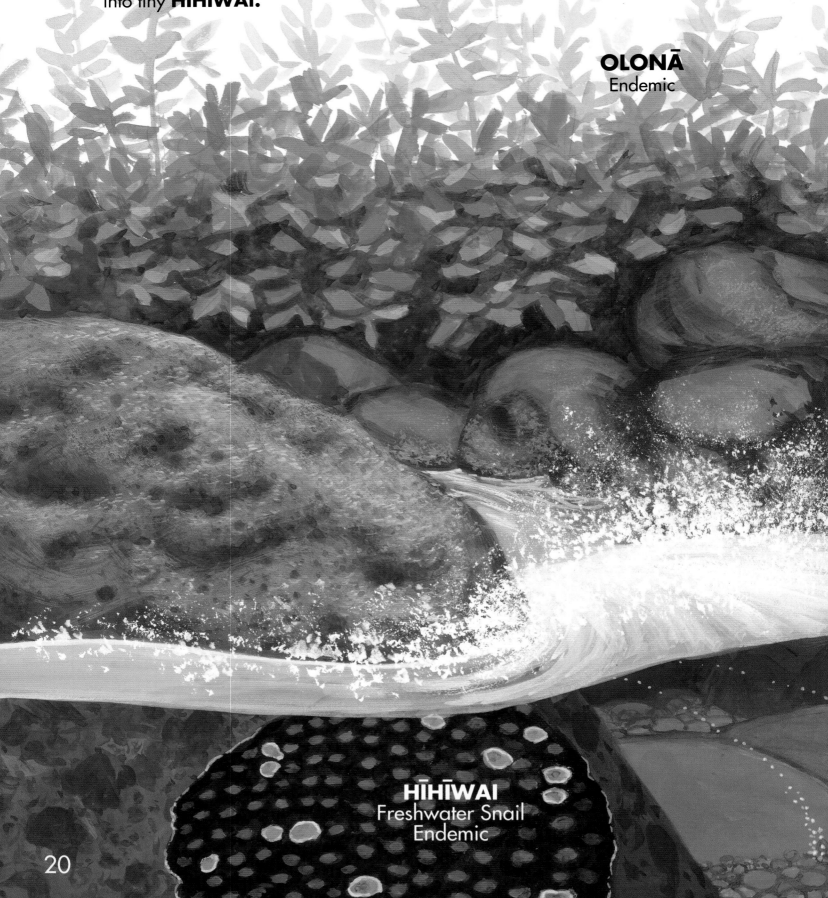

OLONĀ
Endemic

HĪHĪWAI
Freshwater Snail
Endemic

Then they return to the mouths of the streams and begin crawling upstream, where they will live the rest of their lives.

All of Hawai'i's native freshwater fishes and shrimps spend a part of their lives in the sea.

The small, slender tree in the background is the **OLONĀ**. It was an important plant to the Hawaiians because its bark was used to make a strong cord. The cord was used in making fishing nets, feather capes and for many other things.

Larva are young animals in their first stages of life, who often look quite different from what they will become as adults. Larva can change their shape one or more times as they grow up, like a tadpole — which is the larva of a frog.

'O'OPU
Endemic

WAGSTAFF

21

In ancient Hawaiian legends this majestic bird was a symbol of royalty.

It is the **'IO,** our own Hawaiian Hawk.

It is found only on the Big Island of Hawai'i and is often seen soaring in silent circles high above the native forests and pastures, where it hunts insects, rodents and other birds.

The vine you see stretching and spiraling towards the sky is the **'IE'IE.** This vine was another very valuable plant to the Hawaiians, who used it to make fish traps, baskets and sandals. It was also used to weave the **MAHIOLE,** or feathered helmets worn by the chiefs and kings.

'IE'IE
Endemic

Birds brought seeds in their droppings, as well as insects stuck to their feathers or in the mud on their feet. In this way, birds helped scatter life around the Islands.

22

KŌ-LEA-LAU-NUI
Endemic

'IO
Hawaiian Hawk
Endemic
Endangered

WAGSTAFF

It's twilight and the soft yellow glow of the flowers of the **MA'O,** a kind of cotton plant, are beginning to fade.

This is a good time to look carefully for the fluttering shape of our rare Hawaiian bat, the **'ŌPE'A PE'A.** Very little is known about these small bats because they are so hard to find. But we do know that they roost in trees during the day, hunt at dusk for flying insects and closely resemble the Hoary bats found in North America.

HAU KUAHIWI
Endemic
Endangered

MA'O HAU-HELE
Endemic
Endangered

The 'ŌPE'A PE'A and the monk seal are Hawai'i's only native mammals.

24

The ancient Hawaiians used many different things to add color to their **KAPA.**

Some colors came from the soil, but most of them came from plants.
The flowers of the **MA'O** were used in making a green dye.

'ŌPE'A PE'A
Hawaiian Hoary Bat
Endemic
Endangered

MA'O
Hawaiian Cotton
Endemic

This is the **PUEO.** Some ancient Hawaiians worshipped this owl as an **'AUMAKUA,** or a family guardian spirit. Often seen hovering motionless during the day over open grassy areas or near the native forests, it uses its large eyes and ears to find insects and small rodents.

WILIWILI
Hawaiian Coral Tree
Endemic

PUAKALA
Hawaiian Poppy
Endemic

The gnarled tree you see is the **WILIWILI.** The Hawaiians used this tree's light wood for net floats, for surfboards and for the **AMA,** or outriggers, on their canoes. **WILIWILI** is found in hot, rocky places and its bright red seeds are often found along the shore.

PUEO
Hawaiian Short Eared Owl
Endemic

The 'I'O and the PUEO are the only Hawaiian native birds of prey, but fossil remains tell us that other owls, hawks and a Hawaiian eagle lived here long ago. They are now extinct.

27

WAGSTAFF

This dazzling red butterfly is known as the **KAMEHAMEHA** butterfly or **PULELEHUA.** It is named after King Kamehameha the Great, and is found in the native forests, often feeding on the sap of the **KOA** tree.

It is one of only two native species of butterflies that can be found in Hawai'i.

KOA trees are the giants of our native forests. They are used in making the strong, beautiful, ocean-going canoes that the Hawaiians are famous for.

Biologists, scientists who study plants and animals, believe that the **KOA** landed on our Islands early in Hawai'i's natural history because such a large number of native insects make their home in its bark. The **KOA** forests are important to many of these species because they cannot live in any other kind of tree.

Happy Face Spider
Endemic

ULUHE
False Staghorn Fern
Endemic

They are small and most are hardly seen, but there are more than 5,000 different species of native insects in Hawai'i.

28

PULELEHUA
Kamehameha Butterfly
Endemic

KOA
Acacia Koa
Endemic

29

WAGSTAFF

Some birds, like this **KŌLEA,** live in Hawai'i only part of the time.

The **KŌLEA** arrives in Hawai'i around September and will spend the winter feeding on snails and insects. About April, most will begin to change color from tan-white-brown to a black bottom with a bold white stripe. Then they leave Hawai'i and travel north again, flying over 2,500 miles to their cold arctic nesting grounds near Alaska.

The **KŌLEA** usually return to the same area each year, so it's a good chance that the **KŌLEA** you see in a certain place are the same ones that were there before.

KŌLEA
Pacific Golden Plover
Migratory

'ŌHIKI
Ghost Crab
Indigenous

The criss-crossing vines and the delicate flowers of the **PŌHUEHUE** can be found along the hot, sandy shores of many islands. Because its tiny seeds can float, the **PŌHUEHUE** has drifted with the ocean currents and has been spread throughout the Pacific.

PŌHUEHUE
Morning Glory
Indigenous

Biologists believe that about half of Hawai'i's plants began as seeds carried by birds. Migratory birds — those birds that visit Hawai'i from other parts of the earth each year — had a very important part in this.

WAGSTAFF

Along the high slopes of the volcanoes on the Islands of Maui and the Big Island of Hawai'i, and in certain parts of Kaua'i, you will find our State bird, the **NĒNĒ.** This high altitude goose lives on rugged lava flows and is different from other geese because it does not need to live near water. The **NĒNĒ** feeds on berries and other plants.

'ŌHELO
Endemic

NĒNĒ
Hawaiian Goose
Endemic

Endangered

32

The lofty parts of Haleakala volcano on Maui also is the home of the rare and unusual Silversword plant. Its' leaves are covered with silvery hairs that protect it from too much sun and wind and help it to live in the harsh conditions found at the top of the mountain. Just once in its lifetime the Silversword will send up a magnificient stalk full of hundreds of flowers, then it will die.

'ĀHINAHINA
Silversword
Endemic

The NĒNĒ and the Silversword once were close to being extinct, but many efforts and hard work by people to save them are helping them to make a slow recovery.

WAGSTAFF

33

'AMAKIHI
Endemic

he ancient Hawaiian rainforest is the home of many of Hawai'i's special birds, like the **'I'IWI** and the **'AMAKIHI.** These are common birds that can be seen within the forests. Others are rare and very hard to find.

MĀMANE
Endemic

'ŌHI'A LEHUA
Endemic

The feathers of certain birds, such as the **'I'IWI,** were used to make the beautiful feather capes, leis and helmets of the Hawaiian **ALI'I.**

Found growing from the mountains to near the sea, the bright red blossoms of the **'ŌHI'A LEHUA** are a favorite food for many native birds and insects. This graceful tree has an important place in ancient Hawaiian legends, songs and religion.

'I'IWI
Endemic

The 'Ōhi'a Lehua is a good example of how a plant adapted to its surroundings to survive. In windy and dry areas it grows like a short shrub, but in the rainforest it becomes a tall tree, stretching far above the ground.

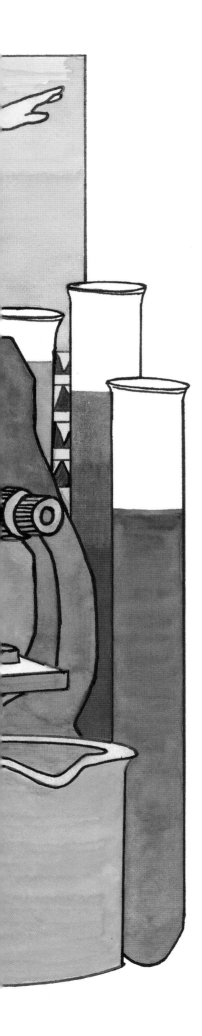

From the tops of the mountains to the depths of the sea, our native plants and animals are a very special part of Hawai'i. Many of them have important places in Hawaiian legends and traditions. Without them, a very large part of our culture would be lost.

Some of them may also hold hidden secrets that could be helpful to mankind in ways we have not yet discovered.

But our native plants and animals are most valuable because many of them can be found only on our Islands and nowhere else on earth. They are the living treasures of our Islands, a link to the past and our natural gifts to the awesome world of life.

We hope that you enjoyed learning about our native plants and animals. Before we leave we'd like to share with you one last thing about them.

Hawai'i has rapidly changed since the arrival of man and many of our native plants and animals are struggling to survive. New plants and animals from other places and the needs of many people have created lots of problems and a fierce battle for food and living space.

38

We are close to losing many of them.
Many are already gone.

39

What will happen to our native plants and animals in the days ahead will depend on the choices we make and the way we choose to behave. All of us must use wisdom in balancing our needs and the needs of other living things.

Each of us can help preserve our native plants and animals. Here are some things you can do:

1. Learn more about our native species by visiting museums, nature centers, botanical gardens and the zoos. Tell others about what you learn.

2. Recycle. This helps us to save resources.

3. Don't litter. Don't Pollute.

4. Don't bring in illegal plants or animals and don't release your pets in the wild. Many of them have caused great damage to our native species. If you see an illegal animal or plant call your local Department of Agriculture office and report it.

5. Aloha 'Āina — Love and respect the land.

Our native plants and animals are rare, priceless, Hawaiian treasures. Few of us have seen many of them, but Punahele and I hope you get to see them all. We also hope that because of our efforts to help preserve them, the future children of Hawai'i and the world will get to see them too.

Aloha.

41

PRONUNCIATION GUIDE

AE'O: EYE-OH

'ĀHINAHINA: AH-HEE-NAH-HEE-NAH

'ĀINA: EYE-NAH

'ĀKOHEKOHE: AH-KOH-HAY-KOH-HAY

ALI'I: AH-LEE-E

ALOHA 'ĀINA: AH-LOW-HA EYE-NAH

AMA: AH-MA

'AMAKIHI: AH-MAH-KEY-HE

'A'O: AH-OH

'ALAE 'ULA: AH-LIE-OOH-LAH

'AUMAKUA: OW-MAH-COO-AH

HALA: HA-LAH

HALEAKALA: HAH-LAY-AH-KAH-LA

HĪHĪWAI: HE-HE-VAI

HONU: HO-NEW

'IE 'IE: E-A-E-A

'I'IWI: E-E-V

'ĪLIO-HOLO-I-KAUAUA: E-LEO HO-LOW E CAH-OO-WOW-AH

'IO: E-OH

'IWA: E-VAH

KAMEHAMEHA: KAH-MAY-HAH-MAY-HAH

KAPA: KAH-PAH

KAUA'I: COW-WAH-EE

KOA: KOH-AH

'KŌLEA: KOH-LAY-AH

KOLOA: KOH-LOW-AH

LANA'I: LAH-NAH-E

LIMU: LEE-MOO

LO'I: LOW-E

MAHIOLE: MAH-HE-OH-LAY

MĀMAKI: MAH-MAH-KEY

MA'O: MAH-OH

MAUI: MAU-EE

NĒNĒ: NAY-NAY

'ŌHELO: OH-HEH-LOW

'Ō HI'A LEHUA: OH-HE-AH LAY-WHO-AH

OLONĀ: OH-LOW-NAH

'ŌPE'A PE'A: O-PAY-AH-PAY-AH

PŌHUEHUE: POH-WHO-EH-WHO-EH

PUEO: POOH-A-OH

PULELEHUA: POOH-LAY-LAY-WHO-AH

WILIWILI: V-LEE-V-LEE

GLOSSARY

ADAPT: A change to a plant or animal that helps it fit into its' surroundings.

FOSSIL: Traces or remains of plants and animals found in hardened sand, soil or rock.

HABITAT: A place where a plant or animal naturally lives.

KAPA: Cloth made from pounding the bark of the wauke or māmaki plant.

LO'I: Taro patches.

MAMMAL: A group of warm blooded animals, with backbones, who breathe air through lungs. They give birth to live young, produce milk to feed them and have fur or hair on their bodies.

POLYNESIANS: A voyaging people from the group of many Islands south of Hawai'i. These people were the first settlers of the Hawaiian Islands.

BIRDS OF PREY: Birds that hunt, kill and feed on other animals.

REPTILE: A group of cold blooded animals, that have a backbone, breathe air and have dry, scaly skins.